Flowers in Praise

*Church Flower Arrangements
and Festivals*

CAPTIONS TO COLOUR PLATES

between pages 48 and 49

York Minster
This tableau, seen in the North nave depicts the Norman Conquest of 1066. The savage prow of a Norman ship is seen riding on a sea of blue delphiniums and bristling grey-green cardoon leaves (Nicholas Servian, Woodmansterne Ltd)

Canterbury Cathedral
Canterbury at Christmas time. Pots of poinsettia plants inserted in tins on a wooden frame were set with variegated holly each side of the nave of pillars before the steps leading to the superb carved stone pulpit which separates the fourteenth century nave from the choir

Durham Cathedral
Group of red flowers in the crypt of the Norman cathedral at Durham, built in forty years (1093–1133)

Salisbury Cathedral
Tall spires of red flowers flanked the tomb of Sir John Cheney who was standard bearer to Henry IV at the Battle of Bosworth. He died in 1509. Cupressus and other greenery was first inserted into the wire netting spires, then metal cones were placed holding the flowers

St Alban's Abbey
Flowers and leaves here rise to fill each recess leaving the seven stone figures which surround the pulpit in full view

Cirencester Parish Church
Interpretive scenes from the life and interests of the people of the ancient town of Cirencester were exhibited during the Festival of Flowers in the parish church. Here, by the west window a charming replica of the Maypole is depicted with colourful posies of flowers

Coventry Cathedral
Yellow eremurus, gladioli, mauve alliums and other flowers were held in a frame which stood in front of the vast wall of clear glass incised with figures of martyrs, angels and saints (Nicholas Servian, Woodmansterne Ltd)

St Paul's Cathedral
This impressive modern terracotta statue of the Virgin and Child in St Paul's Cathedral by Josophena de Vasconcellos was encircled by cream, lemon and tan flowers. In the foreground is one of two colourful floor standing groups which flanked this recess

Flowers in Praise

Church Flower Arrangements and Festivals

Julia Clements

BT Batsford Limited

London

Dedicated to all members of Flower Clubs, Women's Institutes, Townswomen's Guilds, the Council of the Fraternity of the Friends of Abbeys and Churches, and all those who have so lovingly contributed to the design, interpretation and execution of Flower Festivals, depicted in this book, as well as those members of Church Flower Rotas, who continue the work week by week. None are mentioned by name – their work was one of love.

© Julia Clements 1977
First published 1977
New Edition 1979
ISBN 0 7134 3328 0

Filmset by Servis Filmsetting Limited, Manchester

Printed in Great Britain by
The Anchor Press, Tiptree, Essex
for the publishers
BT Batsford Limited
4 Fitzhardinge Street
London W1H 0AH

Contents

Introduction

As I sat, with thousands of others, in Westminster Abbey and listened to the Dean's impressive address on the occasion of the Flower Festival which marked the Abbey's nine hundredth anniversary, I realized that a whole new conception of the living flower world was opening before us.

I listened and stared, sometimes at one particular flower, other times at a whole group, and as I stared, my mind went back to thoughts of the many countries I had visited where flowers had been my only method of communication. The language of the country I often could not speak, the people I did not know, yet the beauty of the flowers and their common language of love helped us to smile at each other and become friends.

Most of us have become conscious over the years of the slogan 'Say it with flowers', whereby even the most tongue-tied can 'voice' emotional messages through the medium of flowers, and here we were on this occasion listening to the message of the flowers which spelled out our thanksgiving for 900 years of continuous worship. The address was moving, yet it was not only in this famous Abbey that the message of love was being communicated to us through flowers, for it was being repeated at various times all over the country, in village, town and city, wherever a Flower Festival was being held.

In the last decade easy travel has familiarized hundreds of thousands of people with the architecture and interior beauty of our churches. The work of these craftsmen has also been brought into our hearts and homes by the media of television and radio.

More and more Festivals are held in churches throughout the year, yet few have fired the imagination and evoked response in so many people, as have the Festivals of Flowers which have been held during recent years all over the country. Flowers have silently told their message in churches large and small, ancient and modern, in addition to those in some of the world's most famous cathedrals, such as St Pauls, Coventry, Salisbury, Canterbury, Durham, York Minster and Westminster Abbey.

In giving thanks with flowers, the scope is wide for the British flower arranger, for no other country has so many ancient churches remaining. There are more

Left Branches of budding blossom or leafy subjects can burst into flower or leaf and then last for weeks in the coolness of a church. Here is an urn filled with crumbled wire netting which held swerving branches of *Philadelphus* (syringa) from which all the leaves were removed. The stem ends were split and warm water was used to which a dessert spoonful of sugar was added

than 10 000 of medieval foundation. Each of England's 16 630 parishes has a church; there are 41 cathedrals, as well as hundreds of chapels. But this book is not intended to describe churches and their history; rather it is written to remind us all of the good work of the devoted members of Flower Clubs, church workers, and the groups of Friends who form rotas to do the flowers each week, all of whom, by their skill and love, have organized these Festivals of Flowers in our churches.

Very little has been written on the true role of flowers in churches. We know that monks grew flowers to place on the altars of the monasteries. I often wonder if we now accept them mainly as adornment. But are they placed as messengers of love? Are they offerings of worship, or are they symbols of purity? Flowers are depicted in so many paintings of the Annunciation, and through the ages have been placed on church altars and tombs, but latterly they seem to have become accepted purely as decoration. And why not? Although ephemeral, when artistically arranged they are worthy of their stand among the carvings, sculptures, paintings and other expressions of art that are to be found in these majestic buildings.

Flower arranging today is much more than placing a few flowers in a jug or vase of water. It has become an art and is practised by tens of thousands of men and women all over the country. Colour and design are subjects now studied in order to obtain the best effects. Settings and architecture also must be considered, and these, coupled with a knowledge of horticulture, enable the flower arranger to illustrate with flowers the colours of the liturgical year (see page 95). But whilst trying always to improve the artistry with which the flowers are arranged, we must never forget that it is the flowers themselves which spell out their message to the masses who come to see them. By consciously being aware of them we can recognize the example they set, for though some are tall and some are short, some are bold and some are shy, and whilst they come in all different varieties and colours, they do not seem to vie with each other for supremacy, neither do they show any jealousies, they just grow to give love and beauty to all who see them.

Some of the most beautiful flower set pieces I have seen have been interpretations of the Scriptures, when plant material of differing shapes, varieties and colour have all been brought into play to tell a story.

I recall the 'History of Flowers' in St Alban's Abbey, a magnificent spectacle which told the story of St Alban, England's first martyr (c 287). Then there was 'Beauty with Reverence' staged in the historic parish church of St Peter in Heysham, Lancashire. Overlooking the sea, this church was celebrating its millenary (967 to 1967). At Exeter Cathedral the theme was 'Building', to honour Bishop John de Grandisson, who died in 1369. He was the last great building Bishop of the Cathedral, and flowers arranged with stone and wood told of his efforts. Brilliant jewel-coloured flowers interpreted biblical texts such as 'And the foundations of the wall of the City were garnished with all manner of precious stones'; also 'And every several gate was one of pearl . . . and the gates of it shall not be shut at all by day: for there shall be no night there.' In Liverpool Cathedral the text 'For God so loved the World' was interpreted with stately lilies, in addition to hundreds of various highly skilled interpretive set pieces depicting the history of the Port and Sherbourne Abbey celebrated its 1200 years of worship with a Flower Festival.

'For All the Saints' was the theme chosen by the church of St Mary Magdalen at Coldean, Brighton. Here the members depicted with flowers and accessories the lives and martyrdom of many of the Saints. An all green arrangement was chosen to represent St Patrick, Patron Saint of Ireland, and lobster pots backed with fishing nets, from which flowed coral and blue flowers and driftwood, to represent St Andrew, the fisherman. St Cecilia, the Patroness of Church Music, was represented by lyrically arranged flowers with sheet music near the organ: and the story of St Catherine, the patroness of young women and wheelwrights, who was tied to a wheel, tortured and finally beheaded, was told in pink and white posies of flowers fixed to a blue painted wheel, at the base of which was a blob of red flowers representing her blood.

Then there was the Herb Festival devised by the Ongar Flower Club when 105 different herbs were used to decorate the oldest wooden church in the world. The church, St Andrews at Greensted-juxta-Ongar in Essex which seats only 80 people, was built of tree trunks in AD 845.

Unusual touches have been seen in many churches such as a complete altar frontal being made of Pampas grass with dry flower motifs and the magnificence that was seen during the 'Beauty for God' Festival of Flowers, in Westminster Cathedral, the centre of Roman Catholicism in London, will forever be remembered for the decorations hanging from every chandelier down the whole length of the nave.

Yet despite these special events, it is in the small churches up and down the country that week by week the beauty of simple flower arrangements is enjoyed; flowers placed by local parishioners, sometimes in jam pots, oft times with wild flowers, but at all times beautiful.

Special flower festivals, however, still are a revelation for many of us who have taken part. We have learned, for instance, that church arrangements should not be too stylized, for this can detract from worship, and except for Festivals, which call for sumptuous feasts, flowers should be used with discrimination and in general should repeat or complement the architectural lines of the church.

Again, apart from special occasions, when the overall theme has to be interpreted, we have learned that it is better to place *light* coloured flowers before a dark background, and to make a *dark* framework of leaves for the flowers if the background be *light*. This dark framework will throw the flowers forward into prominence, whereas had the light flowers been placed against a light background they would not have been seen from the back of the church. Similarly, blue flowers are not a good choice for regular church work, for from a distance they fade into a grey black

9

and lose all impact. Flowers in churches should be loosely arranged with plenty of space between each flower, otherwise if closely packed the result appears from the back of the church as a blob or a mass with no outline.

Of course, at weddings, flowers in colours to complement the bride's or bridesmaids' colour scheme are often used, and schemes to heighten the colours of uniforms, or to interpret various big events being celebrated are frequently used to unify the whole proceedings.

At the back of the book I give hints on the care of flowers and plants for use in churches. I also give some step by step instructions on how to put the flowers in the vases. These I trust will be of help, but this book is really meant to put on record the work of many of us who have taken part in these great events. No names are mentioned, but each, I am sure, will recognize her own. The book is also meant to help all those interested in churches or flowers to pause and become more aware, allowing the flowers to remind us that they are part of the universal plan, and as such possess the same divine spark that is within every living thing. Perhaps these church flower festivals carried out all over the world would encourage more to come in, to look up and, silently, to give praise.

JULIA CLEMENTS
Chelsea, London 1977

Since writing the above, more and more Church Festivals of Flowers have taken place and I am sad that they cannot all be mentioned. However, I cannot let this new edition go to print without including reference to Flowers in Pageantry at Winchester Cathedral, the Silver Jubilee Festival at Westminster Cathedral, and the Jubilee of Flowers at Warwick.

JC 1979

Left   The chapel of St Patrick, Westminster Cathedral, London, decorated for the 'Beauty of God' Festival of Flowers 1976; staged by the Friends of the Cathedral, including some from the Garden Club of America. The colouring was shades of yellow with a little white, about twelve different kinds of greenery and a touch of orange. Amongst the flowers and greenery used, were Molucella, ferns, white 'Bonny Jean' chrysanthemums, yellow and white gladioli, tiny orchids (which had been flown as a present to the Cathedral from Singapore), and the following Lilium: Limelight, Imperial Gold, Green Emerald, Candidum, Enchantment, Golden Clarion and Golden Splendor

Westminster Abbey

Throughout the year of 1966 celebrations under the theme 'One People' were carried out to mark the ninehundredth year of worship in Westminster Abbey for it was here in 1066 that King William was crowned after the Norman Conquest. There had been a church with a small monastery attached to it on this site for some considerable time, but since the crowning of King William (and he chose Westminster Abbey because of his respect for Edward the Confessor who ascended the throne in 1042) it has become closely associated, not only with the Crown, but also with affairs of State.

Every King and Queen of England has been crowned here since 1066 and royal marriages, state openings of parliament as well as burials of kings and famous statesmen all take place in this impressive building so rich in architecture, colour and history.

It was in this magnificent setting that members of the National Association of Flower Arrangement Societies were invited to take part in the ninehundredth anniversary celebrations by decorating the Abbey with flowers. On the following pages are shown some of the hundreds of artistic displays, some large, some small, that were witnessed by tens of thousands on this historic occasion.

It was the Dean who, during his sermon delivered at the Festival of Flowers service at the close of the display, gave the real meaning to the event. I quote from his final passage . . .

'What have we come into Westminster Abbey to see? The flowers? Again I thank you for them and not least those which have been brought from afar, illustrating once more our great 'One People' theme of the Abbey's ninehundredth anniversary.

But we have come to see more than the flowers, more than the beauty of the earth and the wonder of creation. These are the silent messengers which prepare the way for our seeing Him who wonderfully created and yet more wonderfully redeemed. These silent messengers prepare our hearts by faith to see His glory, whose head was crowned not with laurel but with thorns.'

Left   One of the twenty (ten each side) large urns of flowers which stood by the pillars down the whole length of the nave. Starting with deep red, the colour scheme of these groups was monochromatic, reaching a pale peach-pink near the screen. The flowers were held in cones on sticks in wire netting which filled the urns

Above   These huge groups of flowers were placed either side of the sixteenth-century bronze-plated oak gates outside the west end of Henry VII Chapel. The bronze patterns on the doors show symbols of the Tudor dynasty

Right   This huge pedestal group of dried flowers was seen in the north choir aisle near the tomb of Hugo Chamberlain. The colour scheme was beige, brown and gold to complement the carved iron gates

Above Here above the richly coloured tomb of Lord Boucher, standard bearer to Henry V, was placed gold, red and crimson azaleas and acer leaves. The shields, richly painted in green, blue, red and gold, underneath and above the tomb are worth studying

Left This delicate pedestal group of blue delphiniums and cream and yellow lilies was made to match the gold and blue ornamented choir screen at the end of the nave. In the recess of the screen is the statue of Sir Isaac Newton (1642–1727)

Right In the poets corner, the statue of John Dryden (1632–1700) was decorated with beautiful white clematis above, whilst below a swerve of pink and white flowers was laid, all being an interpretation of the affixed quote 'Full blown flower of glorious beauty'

J. DRYDEN.

"Full-blown flower of glorious beauty"

Natus 1632. Mortuus Maij 1. 1700.

JOANNES SHEFFIELD DUX BUC-
KINGHAMIENSIS POSUIT. 1720.

York Minster

York is the largest medieval cathedral in Britain and it is calculated that nearly half of all medieval stained glass which survives in Britain is contained in its 117 windows.

York was a Roman town of great importance – in fact beneath the crypt in the Minster can still be seen the base of a Roman pillar, where in AD 306 Constantine was proclaimed Caesar. It has undergone many changes since that time – the beautiful choir screen, for instance, which is adorned with statues of the Kings of England from William the Conqueror to Henry VI, was built in 1475.

Two magnificent flower pageants have been staged in the Minster by members of the Floral Arrangement Association of the North East of England, to mark the beginning and the end of the restoration programme. Included was an impressive display in the fourteenth-century Chapter House, of copes and vestments rarely seen by the public – each one complemented by a group of flowers.

Nearly 77 000 visitors passed through the West Door during the four days of the last pageant to witness the beauty of the 250 flower arrangements which cannot adequately be described in words. Fitting perhaps, is the simple prayer which was offered by the Archbishop of York at the Service of Thanksgiving. 'God who touches earth with beauty, make my heart anew; with thy Spirit recreate me, Pure and strong and true.'

Left   Multicoloured fresh flower kneelers are here seen placed in front of the beautiful terracotta reredos in St Stephen's Chapel

Above These huge groups in cream, yellow and green, flanked the high altar at the time of the Flower Festival

Right High above one of the exits was this huge floodlit fan of gladioli in peach, pink and crimson

Above Looking down onto the crypt, this brilliant flame and red arrangement of dahlias, gladioli and golden privet was to be seen. The crypt is the site of King Edwin's baptism in AD 627

Right Two groups of flowers were placed high left and low right around the Wentworth monument in the north choir aisle

Salisbury Cathedral

Though not as significant in history as other cathedrals in England, Salisbury is justly famous for its artistic beauty. Rising from the most beautiful setting of any cathedral in England, its slender spire, the tallest in the land, is known throughout the world. The stone spire, 404 feet in height, is of unrivalled beauty and is probably the highest medieval stone spire in the World. The decorated style cloisters, built in 1263–70, are the largest and oldest of any in this country.

The foundation stone of the present cathedral was laid on 28 April 1220, the cathedral being consecrated in 1258. The tower and spire followed in the period 1330–65, the stone for which being carried up by treadmill which is still in position. The spire was struck by lightning in 1559, causing a 60 feet fissure; this was the year after Queen Elizabeth I came to the throne. Since then adequate protection from lightning has been taken.

Many ancient effigies of famous local people and warriors can be seen in the Cathedral, of which the Chapter House, built about 1275, is one of the series of famous octagonal buildings to be found in this country.

The following pages show some of the beautiful flower pieces that were displayed during the Festival of 'Flowers in Glory'.

Page 24   Flowers placed at the base of the nave pulpit

Above Garden flowers in mauve, blue-green and grey were placed high and low to match the tapestry behind the tomb of George Sydenham, Archdeacon of Sarum and Chaplain to Kings Henry VII and VIII

Left Peach and cream flowers were placed on the high ledges of the Audley Chantry which is a characteristic piece of Perpendicular architecture and inside some of the original colouring has been retained

Above   Swerves of flowers held in floral foam were placed each side of this tomb of Bishop Thomas Burgess who was Bishop of Salisbury from 1825–37

Right   Green leaves with white chrysanthemums and auratum lilies and hydrangeas were here arranged in a recess at the end of a portion of the ancient choir screen which dates from 1260

The Twelfth-century font, filled with pale-coloured flowers, was a striking feature of the Festival. The font is made from black Tournai marble carved with reliefs depicting scenes from the life of St Nicholas

Winchester Cathedral

As you enter the West door of Winchester Cathedral the contrast with the exterior severity of the building is both immediate and impressive. More than 1000 years of history is unfolded before you.

The Romans, the West Saxons, the Danes, and the Normans have all left their mark in this magnificent building, which has the longest Gothic nave in Europe. Although the fabric suffered little during the Reformation, at the time of the Civil War many of its treasures were destroyed, statues were torn down and nearly all the stained glass windows were smashed.

At the beginning of the present century the foundations were discovered to be settling which necessitated the tremendous work of underpinning and the building of new buttresses.

In 1977 The Flowers in Pageantry Festival, marking 1000 years of history, was staged by the Wessex Flower Arrangement Association.

Both sides of the stalls in the Lady Chapel were decorated with these delightful arches of dried flowers and glycerined leaves

31

St Paul's Cathedral

On the summit of Ludgate Hill in the City of London, stands St Paul's Cathedral, which having been destroyed by the Fire of London in 1666, miraculously survived the great Fire attack on the City in 1940 during the Second World War.

For thirteen and a half centuries a cathedral dedicated to the honour of Saint Paul has stood on this site for it was here in AD 604 that St Augustine of Canterbury consecrated Mellitus as Bishop of the East Saxons.

The present majestic building is by Christopher Wren, and is the fifth bearing the name of St Paul, the previous all having been destroyed by fire. The cathedral contains the Chapels of two famous Orders of Chivalry, that for the Knights and members of the Order of St Michael and St George, and the Chapel for the Knights and members of the Order of the British Empire, which is at the east end of the crypt.

The crypt said to be the largest in Europe, houses the tombs of the famous, that of Lord Nelson, killed at the Battle of Trafalgar, being sited immediately beneath the centre of the dome. The great dome (68 000 tons), with its whispering gallery, and the eight massive cartoons depicting great events in the life of St Paul (painted by Sir James Thornhill in grisaille) is visited by hundreds of thousands each year.

To decorate this great Cathedral for the Festival of Flowers was the greatest challenge ever accepted by British flower arrangers, who also invited flower arrangers from overseas. The fact that their artistry matched that of the great sculptures, carvings and paintings to be seen in St Paul's, proved they were right to do so.

Left Two large floor standing groups of flowers were placed each side of the magnificent Tigou gates in the south choir aisle

Above Twenty impressive pedestal groups of cream, lemon to gold coloured flowers flanked each side of the nave against the pillars and walls. Similarly coloured flowers held in wrought-iron baskets were hoisted high in the arches

Left Pew end swags of fresh bright red and pink flowers in the chapel of St Michael and St George

Right One of the six dried flower wall swags which were made to complement the work of Grinling Gibbons (1648–1720), many examples of which can be seen in the cathedral

Above This enormous marble font (6½ feet in diameter) made by Francis Bird in 1726 was filled with an all round design of pale lemon, green and cream flowers. *Eremurus* in metal tubes formed the height whilst most of the width was obtained with sprays of green woodpecker gladioli, cream carnations, and green *Molucella laevis* (Bells of Ireland) held firm by crumpled wire netting

Left This assymetrical design in brown and gold was one of two placed each side of the Altar of the American memorial Chapel, which was dedicated by HM The Queen in 1958. Behind are three stained glass windows which are a tribute from the British people to the 28 000 American service men and women who died whilst based on British soil and whose names are inscribed in the great Roll of Honour here. The gold coloured *Eremurus* and lilies backed with stripped lime branches were interspersed with brown glycerined leaves and gilded *Alliums* to match the gilt and brown of the woodwork. The gold vase is by Edward Lutyens

37

Rochester Cathedral

Seven years after St Augustine landed with the Gospel on the Isle of Thanet in Saxon times, Rochester, or Roffa in Kent, entered England's history as a cathedral city. In AD 604 Rochester received its first Bishop. Today in this magnificent building it is possible to see work of every century from the eleventh to the twentieth, and the foundations of the early seventh century Saxon cathedral still lie under the pavement of the nave near the west door.

Although the medieval paintings, the ancient tombs, the splendid sedilia of the fourteenth century, the magnificent Chapter Room doorway (1340), the superbly carved choir screen and other treasures are permanent attractions to worshippers and visitors, it was to flowers the Dean looked for help when he was faced with a vast sum of money for restoration work. At the time of the Flower Festival he wrote 'Flowers and Architecture, each have their own special beauty. The combination of the two gives something more than the aggregate of both. I show some of the many beautiful flower arrangements made by members of the Flower Arrangement Association of Kent together with the lady members of the Rochester Cathedral Flower Guild, who are responsible for the flowers week by week throughout the year.

Left Two huge shields from which flowed gold satin were fixed to pillars each side of the nave; underneath were tall floor standing designs of gold coloured flowers

Above   Pink rubrum lilies, crimson clematis, silver grey rex begonias, leaves and other touches in pink, purple, crimson, and grey were used here to match the altar frontal cloth in the Jesus Chapel

Above right   Small dried flower arrangements were fixed by glue to red felt, which was inserted in each panel of the great pulpit

Right   White flowers and flowing pale blue silk were used in the marble font to convey innocence and purity in baptism. The text beside this design reads 'and when Jesus was baptized he went up immediately from the water and behold the heavens were opened and he saw the spirit of God descending like a dove and alighting on him'. Matthew 3, verse 16

Above This military design of flowers was made to honour those who fell in the Second World War

Left Pillars of red flowers flanked the beautiful white stone high altar designed by Sir Gilbert Scott in 1873. This altar replaces earlier altars which have been pilloried and smashed by warring forces including Cromwell's soldiers

St Alban's Abbey

Overlooking the site of the once famous Roman City of Verulamium, stands the Cathedral and Abbey Church of St Alban. It marks the place where Alban, the martyr, was the first man in England to die for his Faith, some time between 303 and 305. Many of the most beautiful wall paintings in England are to be seen here, among them that of St William of York, the Archbishop in the reign of Stephen (1135–54). It was bricked up for 300 years after the Dissolution of the Monasteries during the reign of Henry VIII (1509–47) but much of the medieval colouring has survived.

The great Norman Tower dominates the landscape for miles around and was built with Roman bricks taken by the Normans in the eleventh century from the ruined pagan City of Verulamium.

One of the most magnificent brasses, that of Thomas de la Mare, is also to be found in St Albans. It is in the chantry chapel south of the presbytery, and was made by a Flemish artist about 1360.

The huge reredos was completed about 1484 by Abbot William of Wallingford; the panel above the altar depicts the Resurrection.

It was against this historic setting of magnificent stonework, paintings, carving that the flowers staged by the Home Counties Association on the following illustrations were photographed.

Left Decorations of pale yellow single spray chrysanthemums were hung on the ends of the choir stalls. Fixed in polythene-covered oasis, no damage can occur to the woodwork

Above One of two large hanging decorations of fruit, berries, leaves and flowers were placed each side of the north entrance of the choir stalls

Left For the Festival, the huge eagle lectern was decorated with garlands of peach and pale green flowers. The 10 feet high pedestal groups by the high altar can be seen in the background

47

Above Pink, crimson and cerise coloured flowers with prunus pissardi foliage were here grouped in a pyramidical style by the large pillars in the nave

Page 49 These large lemon white and green pedestal groups were placed either side of the high altar. Standing on royal blue covered blocks, the flowers, composed of gladioli, auratum lilies, chrysanthemums, hydrangea, love-lies-bleeding, with fatzia and bergenia leaves were all held in wet oasis covered with wire netting

Guildford Cathedral

Standing high on the summit of Stag Hill, just outside Guildford, in Surrey, is the first anglican cathedral to be built on a new site in the South of England since the Reformation in the sixteenth century.

The Foundation Stone was laid in 1936, and although all building was stopped in 1939 when war broke out, it was finally consecrated in 1961, in the presence of Her Majesty Queen Elizabeth II, HRH The Duke of Edinburgh and other members of the Royal Family.

Five years later in 1966 a Flower Festival staged by members of the County of Surrey Flower Arrangement Association was held, which drew thousands up the Hill to this youngest of England's cathedrals.

Left Tapering groups of lemon-coloured chrysanthemums, dahlias and foliage were placed in the arcading in the south ambulatory

Above Towering 15 feet high, two pedestal groups were staged each side of the high altar. Composed of white gladioli, chrysanthemums and lilies, they were backed with pampas grass, green leaves and green *Molucella laevis* (bells of Ireland)

Left This interpretive group of plant material surrounded the huge sculpture of St Francis by John Cobbett

Above   Against a background of red edged with gold, ten shields were decorated with colourful flowers held in plastic covered wet floral foam and hung from the balcony

Right   One of two vertical pedestal groups composed of peach, pink and beige coloured flowers with parchment coloured dried aspidistra leaves and pampas grass, held in gilt urns standing each side of the Bishop's Door

Coventry Cathedral

The beautiful Cathedral Church of St Michael was reduced to ruins during one air raid on the night of 14 November 1940, when Coventry was devastated by the longest one night air raid on any British city during the Second World War. Thousands of people were killed.

The decision to rebuild was made the day after the raid but it was 16 years before the foundation stone was eventually laid. Consecrated in May 1962 in the presence of Queen Elizabeth II, Coventry Cathedral is one of the greatest pieces of modern architecture in the world, and the world now comes to stand in awe and in praise of it.

On entering, one is struck by the mighty tapestry *Christ in Glory* which is the largest in the world being 74 feet in height and 38 feet in width, and replaces the traditional east window.

The glorious silver cross on the High Altar, unlike any other symbolises 'Sacrifice' and the high modern pottery candlesticks, three each side, which are more than 6 feet tall, are believed to be the largest thrown pots in existence.

Both the Coventry Flower Club and later a group of International Florists made their offering with 'Festivals of Flowers' but it was not an easy task to add living beauty to the magnificent works of art such as are to be seen through the wrought iron grill in the Chapel of Christ, the Great Oak Altar, the huge rough hewn boulder font and the gloriously beautiful West Wall of clear glass incised with an array of angels and Saints and never omitting the unexpected sight of the majestic nave windows depicting the Destiny of Man and the Revelation of God.

Gifts came from all over the world to help the resurrection of Coventry Cathedral which is now the centre of the Cathedral Ministry of International Reconciliation; the Cross of Nails made from fourteenth-century hand forged nails, which littered the floor of the burnt out sanctuary, being its symbol.

Left White and yellow flowers were grouped behind and around a 'bird of wing' type piece of carved wood to represent 'Inspiration – the Rising of the New Cathedral' by the Coventry Flower Club

Above Flowers of yellow, blue and white were here placed artistically below the great oak altar in the Chapel of Christ the Servant

Left Red and flame coloured flowers arranged against blackened burnt wood symbolising the destruction of the old cathedral during the Second World War

Right Here flowers are dwarfed by the size of the huge stone boulder hewn out of a hillside, outside of Bethlehem, which is now the Cathedral's font. Thus the most ancient font is to be seen in the most modern Cathedral. It stands in front of the breathtaking blaze of colour for the Baptistry window

Left Many rural pursuits were interpreted to represent the Lancashire countryside. This display by the Lunesdale Flower Club was seen at the entrance to the Chapter House

Left This huge carpet of red flowers was 54 feet long by 6 feet wide and bore the Liverpool coat of arms in red, white and green plant material. It was arranged by the Ulverston and Morecambe Bay Flower Clubs

Liverpool Cathedral

Liverpool Cathedral which stands on St James's Mount overlooking the City was the setting for a magnificent Flower Festival entitled *Finish the Cathedral Fund*. This was organized by members of the Clubs which form the Flower Arrangement Association of the North West. One of England's youngest cathedrals – the Foundation Stone was laid by King Edward VII in 1904 – its architectural grandeur strikes one immediately on entering.

Below *Longiflorum* lilies on the High Altar. The beautiful carved reredos is an integral part of the Great East Wall itself. The Crucifixion is portrayed in the central top panel and below this is a gilded carving representing the Last Supper

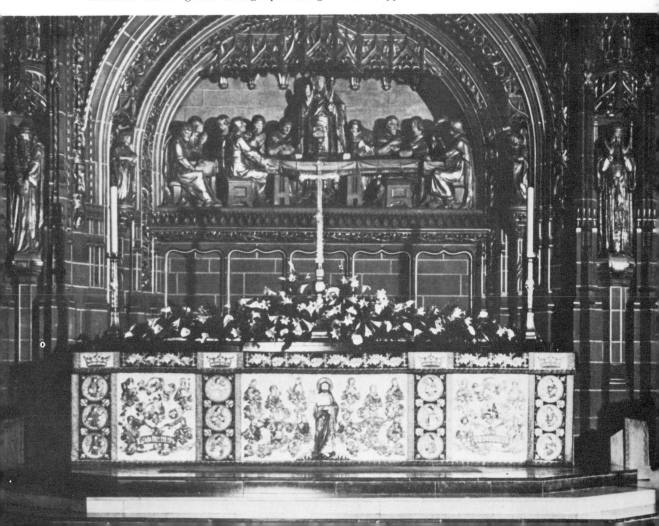

Above   The final touches being put to an enormous cross made out of three thousand red carnations. This was placed on the unfinished Great West Wall of the Cathedral

Left   Lilies arranged around figures of the Nativity

Leicester Cathedral

Below   Garlands of fruit and flowers decorated the columns in the aisles of
Leicester Cathedral

THOMAS BECKET
ARCHBISHOP ∗ SAINT ∗ MARTYR
DIED HERE
TUESDAY 29TH ∗ DECEMBER
1170

Canterbury Cathedral

Canterbury Cathedral the mother church of Anglican Christendom, is the cradle of English Christianity; it is to Canterbury that all Anglican churches throughout the world look as their Spiritual home.

The earliest church is linked with St Augustine, who was sent from Rome by Pope Gregory (597) and who 'recovered' with the aid of Ethelbert, King of Kent, a church built during the Roman occupation of Britain, but in 1067 a fire ruined Canterbury. When Lanfranc became Archbishop in 1070 he set about erecting a more noble Cathedral Church to replace the ruins. Much has happened and many changes have taken place since then but today, the nave, with its seven piers each side, is considered to be the finest product of English Gothic.

History is recorded by the many magnificent monuments to be seen, notably the striking effigy of the Black Prince, the eldest son of Edward III – 1330–76 and in St Gabriel's Chapel can be seen the remains of an early twelfth-century painting but it is to the Martyrdom that most visitors make their way to see the spot where Archbishop Thomas Becket was murdered by four of King Henry II's Knights on 29 December 1170. This book is not meant to describe the history and treasures within the magnificent building but I show just a few pictures of some of the flowers that week by week are lovingly placed within its walls by the members of the Flower Guild, as well as some of the Floral Groups created for the 800th Anniversary of the Martyrdom of St Thomas Becket. Pilgrims have continuously flocked to the Cathedral for centuries to worship at Becket's Shrine only in making your own pilgrimage can the full sense of Canterbury be felt.

Left Kneeler and Bible market in dry flowers, prepared specially for the Becket Festival

Above left Commemorating the 800th anniversary of the murder of St Thomas Becket, symbolic flower arrangements were placed in the Cathedral leading to the spot where he was struck down by four knights of Henry II. Here, near the tablet which records his death were placed red gladioli and red carnations around a black cloak pierced by a sword

TO REMEMBER
SIBELL MARY
COUNTESS GROSVENOR
WITH THANKFULNESS FOR HER LIFE

Chester Cathedral

Above left   This gateway leading to the West Cloister was framed with white flowers and various coloured green foliage

Above right   A Crown for St Werburgh was the title of a Festival of Flowers presented by the Mercia and North Wales Flowers Clubs in Chester Cathedral in aid of the restoration fund

Left   Fruit and flowers here frame the memorial to Sibell Mary, Countess of Grosvenor

Chichester Cathedral

After the Norman Conquest King William ordered that all cathedrals should be moved from small villages to more important centres.

As an alternative to Selsey, some eight miles away, in 1075 the Cathedral of Chichester was established in what had been an important Roman centre.

After a number of setbacks it was finally consecrated in 1184 but three years later a great fire broke out causing serious damage. In a speedy effort to rebuild, some of the old stone weakened by the heat of the fire was used. This is now causing structural weaknesses in this great building, which faces one of the main streets of this old market town, near the coast in the south of England.

Left Tableau in the Royal Sussex Regimental Chapel by members of the Sussex Area of NAFAS

Right The Greeks and the Romans used the leaf form of *Acanthus mollis* for the decoration of the Corinthian column. Hence tall stems of Acanthus were placed behind the bronze replica of the famous cockerel on top of the spire which here stood on broken slabs of stone and columns. Cracks in the walls of this famous Cathedral can be seen. The funds raised were for the Restoration fund. *Acanthus mollis* is a perennial garden plant and dries well *in situ*

Above He who on the cross a victim for the World's salvation bled – Jesus Christ, the King of Glory now is risen from the dead'. An interpretive arrangement of Good Friday and Easter based on Calvary, the Tomb and Resurrection

Right One of the arrangements of flowers and foliage to complement the display of chasubles and copes worn by the priests in processions

Romsey Abbey

King Edward the Elder, son and successor to Alfred the Great, built a church on the site of Romsey Abbey in AD 907. In 1004 the Danes raided this part of Hampshire and the community fled, but some years later they returned and built a bigger stone church. Changes in history has created many changes in the building, especially after it was sold to the parishioners for £100 after the Dissolution of the Monasteries by Henry VIII. However, to raise money for the church rooms building fund the Romsey Flower Arrangement Society organized a Flower Festival which brought thousands of visitors to this ancient and historic Abbey.

Sherbourne Abbey

Left above   Two tall spires of fresh flowers were placed each side of the high altar on the occasion of the Flower Festival

Left below   This beautiful pink, crimson and blue pedestal group of summer garden flowers was set as though framed in this stone recess in the north wall

Below   Picked from the garden, the vicar's wife made this flower group near the side entrance to the choir stalls

Hexham Abbey

Left Hexham Abbey, founded in AD 674, was the scene of a beautiful Flower Festival staged by the Floral Arrangement Association of Northumberland and Durham to raise funds for the renewal of the Abbey organ. Here a series of red and white posies of flowers were staged up the ancient Midnight Stairway to depict the choir descending in their red and white surplices

Below One of the many banners depicting various aspects of the Abbey. Made on a T-shaped wooden background, wet moss was sandwiched between two layers of chicken wire and covered in thin polythene. The surface was then inserted with short green foliage and short flowers formed various patterns this one being of the Rosette window

Cirencester Parish Church

In celebration of one thousand nine hundred years of civic history in Cirencester, the Parish Church, one of England's largest, was decorated with flowers in 1945 by members of Flower Clubs of the South West Area.

This historic church first appeared in the then Roman town of Corininium (c 300). Later burnt by the Saxons it was rebuilt by them in the year 700. After the Norman Conquest (1066) this Saxon church was demolished in 1117 and a Norman church was built on the present site. It has gone through all kinds of rebuilding and additions since then and even survived the dissolution of the Abbey in 1539 when this part was demolished by Henry VIII. Today it stands proudly as the lofty tower dominates this ancient market Town.

Left Red, yellow and flame coloured flowers were placed in the monument to George Monox, Sheriff of London in the time of Charles II (1630–85)

Below left The fourteenth-century font is seen here arrayed with simple marguerites

Below An arrangement of yellow roses and daisies clipped over every pew end

Bangor Cathedral

Above left   Tribute of Eire to the Pilgrimage of Flowers celebrated in Bangor Cathedral

Above right   Coat of Arms made in seeds of HRH Prince of Wales shown during the Pilgrimage of Flowers in Wales

78

USHAW COLLEGE
NORTHUMBERLAND

An impressive arrangement of lilies on the high altar in St Cuthbert's Chapel, Ushaw College, decorated by members of the Northumberland and Durham area

GREAT SOMERFORD
PARISH CHURCH

This small village church in Wiltshire, the home of Captain Mark Phillips, husband of Princess Anne, was decorated with flowers to raise the money for the reparation of the bells so that they could be rung with joy on the occasion of the Royal Wedding. I show one of the decorated outside pillars

ST LUKE'S CHURCH CHELSEA

In the Chelsea Parish Church of St Luke a Flower Festival was held to raise funds to help restore the roof. In this marble font pink rhododendrons, foxgloves and white paeonies were massed with pale green leaves. It was in this Gothic styled church that Charles Kingsley, author of *The Water Babies* and *Westward Ho!* was for a time curate, during the incumbency of his father (1836–60)

ST KESSOG'S, AUCTERARDER

White delphiniums, yellow roses and carnations with variegated foliage were here grouped for the Flower Festival by members of Crieff and District Flower Clubs in St Kessog's Church in Aucterarder, Scotland

WESTMINSTER
CATHEDRAL

The 'Avenue of Peace' given by the Dutch
on the occasion of the Festival of Flowers
when 64 other nations sent flowers to mark
our Queen's Silver Jubilee

SHERSTON CHURCH
GLOUCESTERSHIRE

Two thousand years of village history was
celebrated with flowers in the Sherston
team of churches in Gloucestershire. This
design is 5 feet high. It consists of gilded
lotus pods, coco spathes and pipes with
sheet music illustrated by blackened teazles
commemorated the restoration of the Sherston Church organ, the text reading 'Each
jubilant chord re-echo around. Loud organs
His glory forth tell in deep tone'

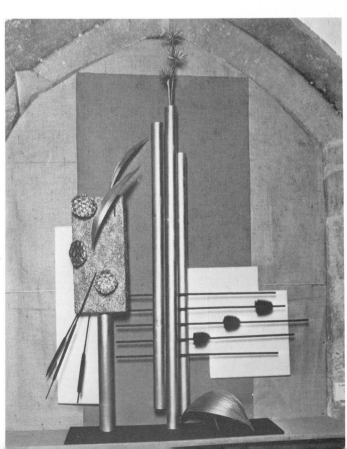

KNIGHTON CHURCH, RADNORSHIRE

The members of the Church Flower Guild at Knighton, Radnorshire, meet regularly to plan the flowers that adorn their church. This delightful group of white blossom, white snowdrops, yellow daffodils and primroses with a basket of eggs on a moss covered bark base is a reminder of the symbolism of the egg to the early Christians. It also proves that simple flowers can be as effective as a mass display

DALKEITH CHURCH

Lilies and carnations in flame and yellow are here seen grouped by the pulpit in the Kirk of the Canongate in Dalkeith, Scotland

Left Collegiate Church of St Mary, Warwick, white and gold flowers complementing the colours of this cope and chasuble, arranged for the celebration of their Jubilee of Flowers, staged by the Warwickshire Flower Clubs

Practical Hints

Drawings by Margaret Davies

Many visitors to Britain have stood in awe before the wonderful spectacle of some of the Church Festivals of Flowers. Others in smaller churches have raised the beauty of the simple flowers themselves. Still others, planning their own Festival of Flowers have wondered how the flowers are kept in place.

Every church has different architecture, so in many cases the mechanics for holding flowers are fashioned to suit each particular setting. However, I hope the following drawings will help those anxious to try for themselves.

Each style can be made bigger or smaller to suit the needs of most backgrounds, but whatever artifice you make to hold the flowers in place, do make sure that enough water can be held to keep the flowers fresh and that a team of helpers are gathered to fill up with water each day of the Festival, removing any wilting flowers, replacing them with fresh ones.

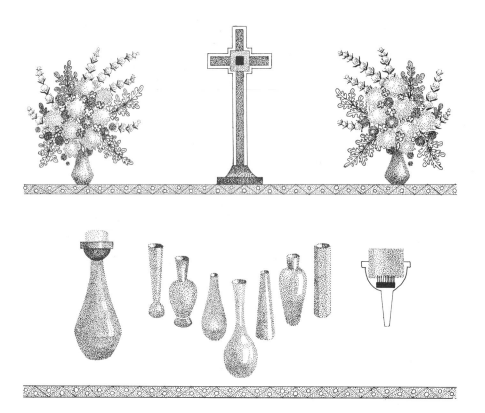

Altar

1 Get 4 or 6 narrow tins or plastic containers and stand one behind and one in front of the cross with 1 or 2 each side, according to length of decoration required. Fill with wet Oasis pressed on to a pin holder – this avoids toppling over

2 Flowers should be inserted slightly taller in the centre near the cross, spreading out lower at sides, with trails, Sometimes advisable to stand cross on a box to give greater height

85

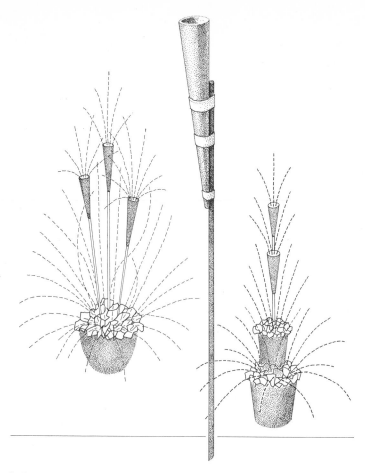

Above   Left – use 1 or 3 metal cones fixed to sticks with Sellotape to obtain greater height for flowers in large pedestal groups. Insert these in the container first. Right – a tall narrow floor standing group can be achieved by standing one vase inside another, adding crumpled wire netting and two metal cones

Right   *For mass pedestal group in church*

Step 1   Place a large pinholder in the base of the bowl and press on to it a block of floral foam (Oasis) well soaked in water. Cover this with a piece of crumpled wire netting which will support heavy stems and avoid the foam breaking up. Allow the foam to reach about two inches above the rim of the container. Then insert the tall, thin stems to form a triangular pattern, making sure the lower front stems protrude forward.

Step 2   Insert the stronger, more dominant flowers down the centre, below each other, the lower ones protruding forward over the rim

Step 3   Fill in with less important flowers working from top to base and from outside to centre inserting them always to a central point underneath the tallest stem. Unite all these stems around the centre with some larger leaves, and finish by adding trailing stems say of ivy, to unite the flowers to the pedestal. Add leaves flowing backwards to avoid a flat effect

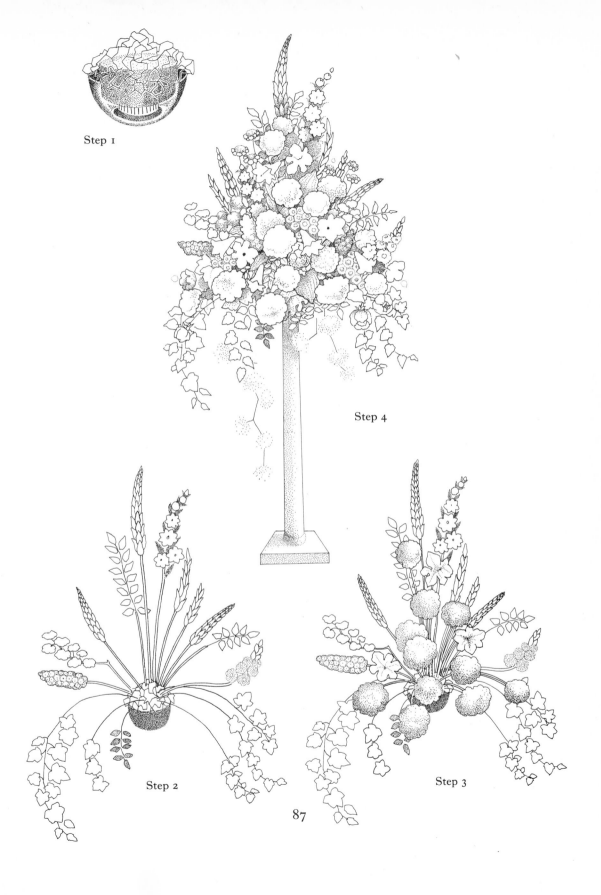

Step 1

Step 4

Step 2

Step 3

87

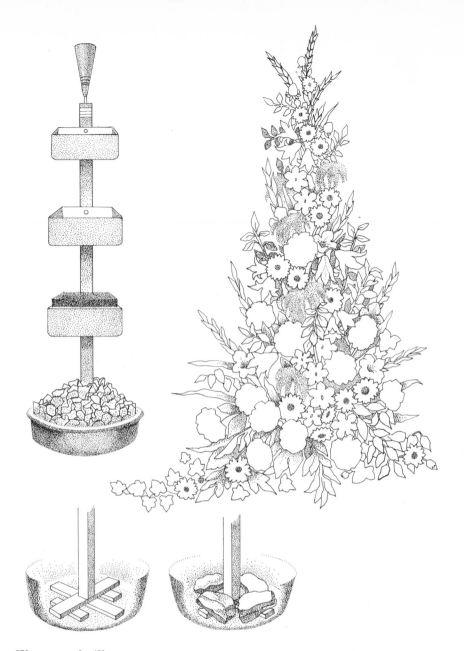

Floor stand pillars

Screw 2 pieces of baton 22 cm (9 in.) long crosswise to the base of a tall broom handle or strong baton, to the height required and stand this in the base of a green tin tray or washing up bowl. Make it stable by weighing down with stones and add wet Oasis covered with wire netting, to hold the lowest heavy flowers. Fix 2 or 3 tins or plastic food containers at different heights to the baton and fill with floral foam. Add a cone at the top if a more pointed effect is required. Allow flowers to flow out a little at the base to hide the container, the rest can be placed upwards and outwards each level just covering the other and covering the tin

Kneelers

Fill a shallow baking tin or plastic seed tray with well water-soaked Oasis, allowing it to reach just above the rim. Cover the rim with greenery pointing downwards, then insert short flowers in any desired pattern

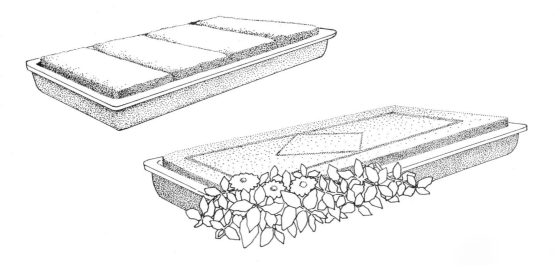

Different patterned kneelers made of dry and fresh flowers were intermingled with woven tapestry ones to form this carpet leading to the altar at Sherston Church, Gloucestershire

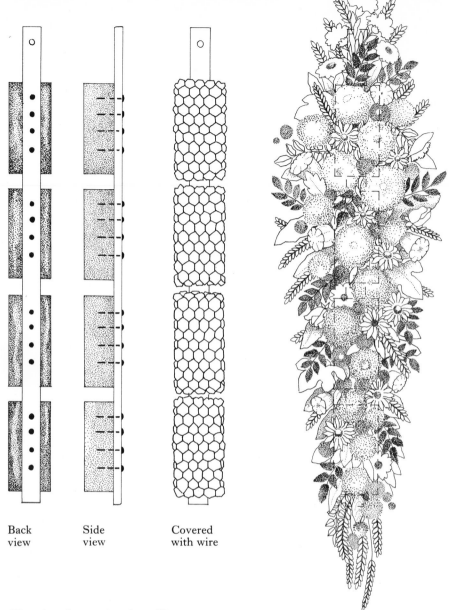

Back view   Side view   Covered with wire

Hanging decoration for pillar

Step 1   Use a 5 cm (2 in.) wide lathe of wood of a desired length and insert nails, on the reverse side. Cover blocks of Oasis (floral foam) with thin plastic, and press these on to the nails. If heavy flowers are to be used cover the plastic with wire netting, for extra support

Step 2   Insert the flowers and leaves in any desired pattern, making the emphasis either at the top or in the middle. These can be made with dry or fresh flowers. If the latter it might be wise to add an extra piece of plastic at the base to catch any water that might drip

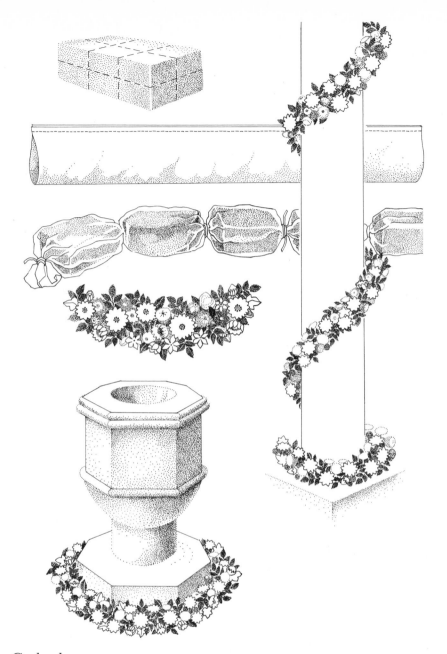

Garlands

These can be used to encircle the tall pillars or the base of statues or doorways, pulpits, lecterns and fonts

1 Stitch by machine long narrow strips of thin plastic sheeting and insert small blocks of water-soaked Oasis. Tie with wool or string here and there to create a string of sausage like effect, which enables it to bend around any structure

2 Insert short flowers, making holes in the plastic first with knitting needle. Spray with water

Care of cut flowers

Nothing is more disappointing than to see a beautifully executed flower arrangement falling out of shape and position because the flowers and leaves have started to wilt. This need never happen if you take care of your plant material *before* you make the arrangement and then look after it daily if you can. There is little truth in the saying that some flowers do not live well with others, just as the adage that aspirins or pennies in the water will help them live longer. Of course aspirins will help kill bacteria, which, if present around the cut stem ends, certainly tends to shorten the life of the bloom, but failing aspirin, a few spots of clear disinfectant will do equally well or, better still, something I always use is a tablet of charcoal dropped into the base, as this will absorb the poisons.

So, when making flower decorations for the church which you trust will last a week, here are a few tips which I have found invaluable.

1 Always buy or pick your flowers the day before you intend to arrange them. Recut the stems and leave in deep water overnight, so that the water channels become fully charged.
2 All leafy twigs and flat surfaced leaves should be submerged over night in water, adding a teaspoonful of sugar to a quart of water as this will place a slight film over the pores of the leaves on the underside and so avoid loss of moisture through transpiration. The exception to this is the grey woolly type of leaf.
3 Before doing either of the above, split the stem ends of all woody plants, such as roses, lilac, and leafy and flowering shrubs.
4 Have warm water in the vase before placing your flowers. If using a flower foam, be sure that it is well soaked through and whether using crumpled wire netting or floral foam, do leave a space at the back to allow water to be added each day.

Pew ends (right)

1 Make holes in one end of plastic food containers to take string or wire for hanging and fill with wet Oasis. A strip of Sellotape across the front will hold the Oasis in place. Then insert flowers, flowing downwards or in any desired style
2 Similar to hanging pillar decoration, but smaller
3 Screw a small tin or plastic food container to a broom holder. Fill with Oasis, then press on to top of pew end and arrange flowers. If a colour emphasis down the whole length of the church is required, screw the tins first to similarly painted or covered boards, then screw the board to the broom holder and press on. Pour sealing wax or melted candle wax over screw joints to effect water tightness

93

5 If using metal cones to heighten the design do not forget to fill them with water or wet floral foam.

5 Sugar in the water will help most flowers to last with the exception of daffodils and narcissi which exude a sticky substance.

6 Most flowers last longer if the lower leaves are removed, for they are inclined to take up the water before it reaches the flower at the top.

7 If flowers are delivered or arrive by post in a wilted state recut the stem ends and stand in very hot water and leave until it cools. This does not apply to soft stemmed flowers such as tulips.

8 When buying tulips, cut off the white stem end, they only drink through the green ends.

9 Hellebores including, Christmas roses and those with similar stem structures, will benefit if a pin or needle is dragged down the side of the stem making a slight split then stood in deep warm water, adding a little sugar.

10 Delphiniums and other hollow stemmed flowers will benefit if warm water is poured into the hollow stem, then plugged with cotton wool. This may appear fussy, but it pays to see your stately delphiniums, still standing stately after days with this treatment.

Experiment yourself with any items I have not mentioned but remember (1) that all flower stems should be recut and left in deep water before using; (2) most leaves should be submerged for hours or over night before using; (3) split all woody stemmed twigs or flowers; (4) have warm water in the container before starting the arrangement and top up each day.

Liturgical colours

The following will give the general Use of Liturgical Colours in the Church of England at the present time.

VIOLET is used on:

    all Vigils, Ember Days (except the Trinity Ember Days), also in Advent and Lent.

    Blue is sometimes used instead of violet.

    Passion Red is also used from Passion Sunday until Maundy Thursday.

    Unbleached linen is also used in Lent.

WHITE or 'THE BEST' is used on:

    all festival seasons except Whitsuntide, ie from Christmas Day until the Octave of Epiphany, from Easter Day until the Eve of Pentecot and on Trinity Sunday.

    It is also used on all feasts of the Virgin Mary and of saints who are not martyrs and on All Saints Day. In some places a mixture of white and red is used on All Saints Day.

    It is also used on St John the Baptist's Nativity but red on the feast of his beheading.

    It is also used on the Feast of the Dedication or Consecration of a Church and Thanksgiving for Harvest, and at the Solemnization of Matrimony.

RED is used at:

    Whitsuntide and on feasts of Martyrs.

    Churches which possess Passion red as well as the red associated with Whitsuntide may suitably use the Passion red for martyrs and the Whitsun red for apostles.

GREEN is used:

    from the Monday after the first Sunday after Epiphany until the Eve of Septuagesima and from the Monday after Trinity Sunday until the Eve of Advent Sunday.

Architectural periods

Saxon	7th Century to 1066	
Norman	1066 to 1189	Romanesque
Transitional Norman	1145 to 1189	
Early English	1189 to 1280	
Decorated	1280 to 1377	
Perpendicular	1377 to 1547	Gothic
Early Tudor	1500 to 1547	
Late Tudor	1547 to 1603	
Stuart (Jacobean earlier in the period and Carolean later)	1603 to 1689	Classical
Hanoverian (William and Mary, Anne and Georgian)	1689 to 1837	

Saxon

Early English

Early Tudor

Norman

Decorated

Late Tudor

Hanoverian

Transitional

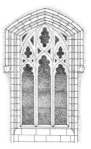

Perpendicular

Stuart